MW00949221

Amazing Archaeology

Pompeii

by Julie Murray

Dash!
LEVELED READERS
An Imprint of Abdo Zoom • abdobooks.com

Level 1 – Beginning
Short and simple sentences with familiar words or patterns for children who are beginning to understand how letters and sounds go together.

Level 2 – Emerging
Longer words and sentences with more complex language patterns for readers who are practicing common words and letter sounds.

Level 3 – Transitional
More developed language and vocabulary for readers who are becoming more independent.

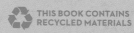
THIS BOOK CONTAINS RECYCLED MATERIALS

abdobooks.com

Published by Abdo Zoom, a division of ABDO, PO Box 398166, Minneapolis, Minnesota 55439. Copyright © 2022 by Abdo Consulting Group, Inc. International copyrights reserved in all countries. No part of this book may be reproduced in any form without written permission from the publisher. Dash!™ is a trademark and logo of Abdo Zoom.

Printed in the United States of America, North Mankato, Minnesota.
102021
012022

Photo Credits: Granger Collection, iStock, Shutterstock
Production Contributors: Kenny Abdo, Jennie Forsberg, Grace Hansen, John Hansen
Design Contributors: Candice Keimig, Neil Klinepier

Library of Congress Control Number: 2021940209

Publisher's Cataloging in Publication Data

Names: Murray, Julie, author.
Title: Pompeii / by Julie Murray
Description: Minneapolis, Minnesota : Abdo Zoom, 2022 | Series: Amazing archaeology | Includes online resources and index.
Identifiers: ISBN 9781098226688 (lib. bdg.) | ISBN 9781644946411 (pbk.) | ISBN 9781098227524 (ebook) | ISBN 9781098227944 (Read-to-Me ebook)
Subjects: LCSH: Pompeii (Extinct city)--Juvenile literature. | Italy--Antiquities--Juvenile literature. | Civilization, Ancient--Juvenile literature. | Architecture, Roman--Juvenile literature. | Excavations (Archaeology)--Juvenile literature. | Archaeology and history--Juvenile literature.
Classification: DDC 937--dc23

Table of Contents

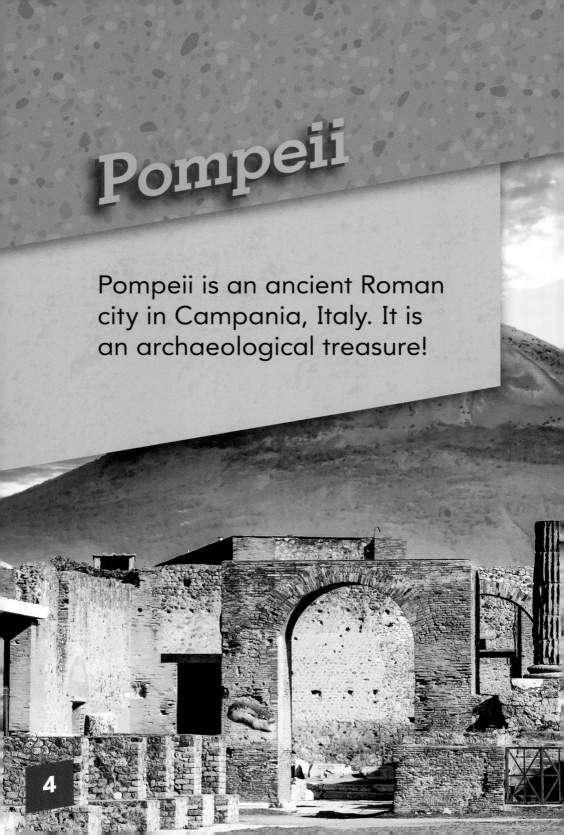

Pompeii

Pompeii is an ancient Roman city in Campania, Italy. It is an archaeological treasure!

GERMANY

SWITZ.

AUSTRIA

FRANCE

ITALY

Pompeii

The city and some of its people were buried in **volcanic ash** nearly 2,000 years ago.

Before the eruption, Pompeii was a **thriving** city with about 15,000 residents. It had a busy market, and even barbershops. But it was best known for its **agriculture**.

9

The Eruption

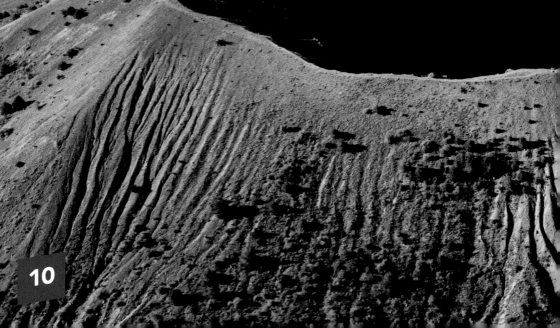

Pompeii was near Mount Vesuvius, a very powerful volcano.

On August 24, 79 CE, Vesuvius erupted with great force. Ash flew more than nine miles (14.5 km) into the air.

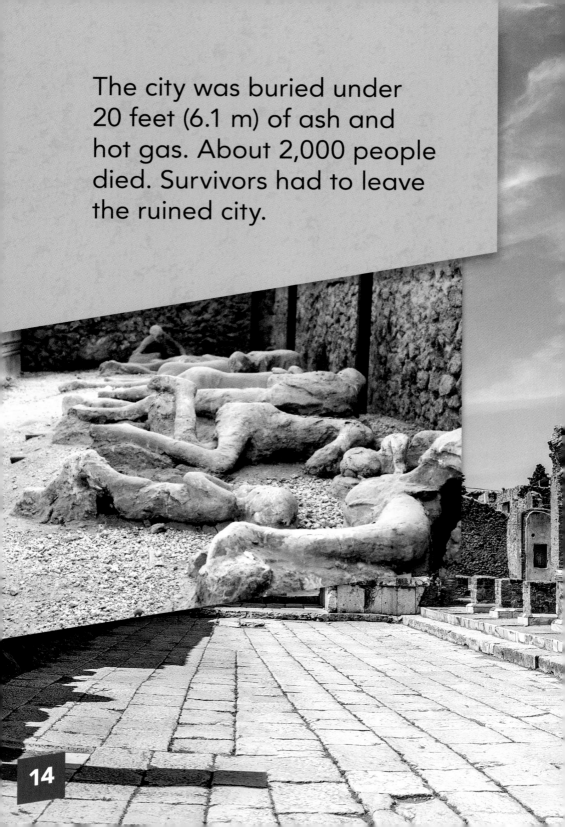

The city was buried under 20 feet (6.1 m) of ash and hot gas. About 2,000 people died. Survivors had to leave the ruined city.

15

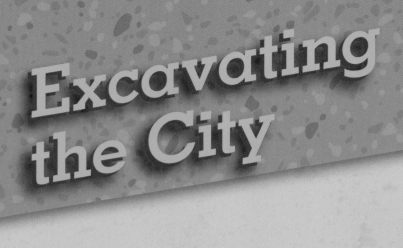

Excavating the City

Pompeii was mostly undisturbed until 1748. Then, a group began excavating the site. They found preserved artifacts that were buried in the ground.

Ancient Roman art, coins, statues, and pottery were found in the hardened ash. Temples, **Roman baths**, and other buildings were uncovered. Some of the people who perished were also found.

Today, about two-thirds of the city has been revealed. People can tour Pompeii. They can feel what life was like in an ancient Roman town.

More Facts

- **Archaeologist** Giuseppe Fiorelli's way of excavating is credited with preserving Pompeii.

- Plaster casts of the human remains found at Pompeii were made. These can be seen at the site today.

- Pompeii is a World Heritage Site. More than 2.5 million people visit each year.

Glossary

agriculture – the science and work of raising crops and farm animals.

archaeologist – a scientist that digs up and then studies objects such as pottery, tools, and buildings. Archaeology is the study of past human life.

Roman bath – a complex with bathrooms and a cold bath used for cooling off.

thriving – doing well or being successful.

volcanic ash – fragments of rock, minerals, and volcanic gas created during volcanic eruptions.

Index

Online Resources

Booklinks
NONFICTION NETWORK
FREE! ONLINE NONFICTION RESOURCES

To learn more about Pompeii, please visit **abdobooklinks.com** or scan this QR code. These links are routinely monitored and updated to provide the most current information available.